The Feels

Pandemic on the Brain
One Private Practice's Perspective

Cory Nicolas, LMHC

Family Tree Project LLP

DEDICATION

This book is dedicated to my father who taught me two things that keep me sane, fishing and soccer. Most importantly, he taught me that it's not what you do, but who you are as person and a human, that is the path to greatness. This book is also dedicated to the clinicians and clients who have contributed to the knowledge, growth, and the impact that Family Tree Project has had on the community.

CONTENTS

ACKNOWLEDGMENTS

I would like to acknowledge the Hawaii National Guard Youth Challenge Academy for allowing us to continue our work with their Youth with Promise.

I would like to acknowledge the Staff, Students, and Past Partners of Family Tree Project, both past and current. The work we do is exceptional, because of exceptional people. I am also blessed with my current business partner, Jessica Torralva, who keeps me grounded but is always willing to go for the ride.

I would like to acknowledge my family and friends; without their support I would be a hot mess. It was a difficult two years, and I want to acknowledge all of you who helped me through my dad's passing, especially my Hilo Posse. I am blessed with two besties (Val and Stacey) who will always have my back. It is because of them, I am never afraid to fall. My husband, Zan and Shan and Shawna-Lynn have always been my "why". My safety net is large and strong because of all of you.

1 INTRODUCTION

Growing up in Hawaii, in a local and Asian culture, I was taught to mask my feelings. I remember moments growing up when I was told "stop crying, or I will give you something to cry about." As I parent, I remember repeating this in frustration with my own kids when they were younger. This created a belief that what you are feeling is not valid, and It is not okay to feel or show emotion. However, as a therapist, I have learned that stopping and burying the emotion creates more dysfunction. Crying or showing emotion has the perception of vulnerability and weakness, similar to my own life lessons. I know this now to be untrue. To sit in your negative memories and face the source of your negative cognitions is an empowering moment and takes courage.

As a trauma therapist, I use techniques such as Brainspotting and Eye Movement Desensitization Reprocessing (EMDR) to help clients activate traumatic events connected to negative beliefs about themselves. These modalities are trauma-focused and trigger traumatic memories and the negative cognitions attached to trauma.

Both modalities bring past trauma to the forefront to allow the client to reprocess the event and separate the trauma from the cognitions.

I sit with clients as they "sit in it" and force themselves to re-live these events, reprocess, and disconnect themselves from the negative beliefs. I have been doing this for a few years with many positive results. In training, we are told to teach our clients to compartmentalize these emotions and memories when they are activated or triggered outside of the therapeutic environment. I have a different insight now, I feel we can use the same format in our everyday lives to process if we just allow the "feels" to happen.

Earlier this year, my father contracted COVID. He was in the hospital for a month before they decided to put him on the ventilator. He never improved and was put in a secondary hospital with the hope of weaning him off the ventilator and waking him up. The doctors told our family that he lost brain function and was possibly brain dead. My siblings and I were constantly in conflict over what should be done. At this point, there was a lot going on. I had been away from home for 4 months in Vegas, taking care of my mom. I knew my dad was dying and I was frustrated and stressed over the entire situation. I never allowed myself to cry. I would avoid conversations so that I didn't get triggered as I felt I had to be strong for my mom. Eventually, the stress got to me and one morning I woke up with no eyebrows. My stress response as I was trying to hold it together, resulted an unconscious compulsive reaction. Basically, I pulled all my eyebrow hairs out one by one, without even realizing that I did it.

I panicked that morning. What would my online telehealth clients think of their therapist now with no eyebrows? I ran to the store to purchase an eyebrow pencil, but it was difficult to apply, as I have only worn makeup on a few occasions. My cousin referred me to a professional micro-blader (which turned out to be a painful experience), but I had eyebrows again. As a result of this experience, I realized I needed a therapist myself, and was lucky to find an excellent one. She gave me a voice and allowed me to feel my emotions, but I still avoided deep emotions. I found distractions of current stressors to talk about in my sessions rather than talking about my dad and my fears of his passing.

Eventually, my fears were realized as the hospital decided there was nothing they could do for him, and the only choice was hospice. The night before we were taking him off the ventilator, I prayed that God would somehow grant us a miracle. I remember praying that my dad would wake up and provide us with the guidance we needed. That morning, my brother texted to say that my dad was conscious. We rushed to the hospital. He was mostly paralyzed. He couldn't seem to move his left side and could only slightly move his right hand. However, if you lifted his eyelids up for him, he could see and when asked questions, he could nod his head for yes or no. He confirmed that he didn't want to live on a ventilator, and he wanted to go to hospice. For a moment, I was alone with him. As in most Japanese families, we never verbally tell each other that we loved each other, it was always just known. For the first time in my life, I told my dad that I loved him and how much I would miss him. I started to cry, but my old self was trained to hold it back. My dad died later that day, but I did have some relief that I got to say what I felt.

I came home and resumed my practice. Still in survivor mode, I immersed myself into work. My practice has a partnership with the National Guard Youth Challenge Academy. This program is a 5-month residential program for youth with promise that come from diverse backgrounds but struggle with many disparities such as anger, anxiety, and depressed moods. I work closely with the female population, as they have the most anger issues and combined with their carbonated hormones are easily triggered by each other. One of the clients that I worked with was an 18-year-old girl. She stated that she was feeling home sick and at night she cries silently to herself in bed. As a counselor, I validated her feelings and told her crying is a normal reaction to missing home. I told her that nothing is wrong with feeling sad. I encouraged her to lock herself in the bathroom one night and just allow herself to "ugly cry" until there were no more tears. The next day, she shared with me that she did as I suggested. She shared how she allowed the thoughts and beliefs to overcome her, and she cried until she felt "empty." Her response was then, "Ma'am, I totally felt better after." It was in that moment, I realized I was onto something. I said out loud, "maybe when you don't allow yourself to feel what you feel, you prolong the suffering, and it turns into anger." This was a huge insight and felt that it resonated with her. I realized that she just went through re-processing on her own. Something so simple, that blew my mind wide open.

My friend Dell often sends me random TikToks of videos that she feels I will relate to. Over the weekend, she sent me a TikTok of this girl singing a song with the point of view from someone who had passed. I was in bed that morning alone, I listened to the song and automatically tried to hold the tears back. Then I realized what I was doing and forced myself to sit in it. I "ugly cried" for the first time in years, until the tears stopped. As I listened to the song, the memories of my dad flashed through my mind and allowed myself to feel it. Then when I was "empty", I washed my face and went on with my day. It was a good day. Now I realize, if I want to move forward and be functional, I must face and sit in the emotion rather than hide from it. This was the beginning of my new process.

2 DUMBING DOWN THE SCIENCE

As a therapist, I worked for a few years seeing the long-term effects of talk therapy, but I always searched for different answers and finding an effective black and white solution. I found EMDR and Brain spotting that allowed me to challenge trauma, help clients reprocess it, and watch the disparities decline and the resilience emerge. In this quest, I found an entire new perspective based on Adverse Childhood Experiences (ACEs). I will not go into detail about this Kaiser study that has changed the face of trauma as that would make this read boring. You can become a google warrior and find that info on your own.

Basically, Adverse Childhood Experiences are traumatic moments from utero to age 21 (brain growth) that measure abuse or neglect, or a perception of an unsafe and unstable environment. Based on the Kaiser study, it is scale of ten. The higher the score the more likely it would be for a person to have disparities. I believe that ACEs are not specific to those ten questions but include any traumatic moment in which someone did not feel safe.

However, I simply explain it as three main components of your brain that relate to the scary or "crappy" stuff that happen to you as you grow up. The Frontal lobe, the Amygdala, and the Hippocampus.

The frontal lobe is the front part of the brain, and it holds your feelings, your personality, and is also where you make good decisions. When this is not working properly, you tend to make impulsive choices. I always ask my clients these three questions:

> "Do you ever make a decision and then immediately regret it and wonder: "Why in the 'F' did I do that?"

> "Do you have a hard time sleeping and often overthink things?"

> "Do you sometimes feel sad and have no idea why you feel sad and then it makes you sadder?"

The answers are always yes, and I let them know that this is their frontal lobe that's gone haywire.

The Hippocampus is like the computer of your brain. Your brain processes memories like your computer processes files.

> *I listen to a soft rock station in my car and every once in a while, it will play a song from the 80's. A while back I heard Run DMC song, "You be Illin" and it brought back a memory of when I was a freshman in high school and I had a sleepover with my friends and we were blasting this song and pathetically tried to rap along to the lyrics.*

That is my hippocampus working as this was a positive memory that was filed in my brain. However, when the hippocampus is not working properly, it looks like an unorganized desktop home page, with files scattered all over. The only positive thing about having files on your desktop home page is the easy access, you don't have to search through all your organized files to find it. This works negatively with your brain, the memories that aren't filed correctly get easily accessed and may not be a feel-good experience.

The Amygdala is the panic button. When something is perceived as a threat, it activates the fight, flight, or freeze response. It reminds me of going to a haunted house. In my head, I know it's fake and it's just people behind the mask, but this still causes me to get activated. As I walk around the corner through the dark, my heart is racing, anxiety is at a high level and I'm just waiting for something to jump out at me. When the scary costume appears, my reaction is to do all three, I freeze first, I scream, and then I punch the poor guy. Imagine your entire life growing up and feeling like you're walking through a haunted house? Just as if you keep pressing a button it's eventually going to get stuck.

When the amygdala is activated, it shuts down the link to the frontal lobe. Good decisions become impossible to make, and quick impulsive judgments take place. The immediate response is anger or sadness. There is truth to the rule of not making big decisions when you are upset, it is literally impossible according to science.

I have two daughters who are close in age. Imagine having two daughters in puberty in one house at the same time. There is a lot screaming "I hate you" or "I can't wait to move out" and slamming doors becomes an everyday occurrence. I should be given an award for successfully surviving two girls in puberty at the same time. During their high school years, I was always activated. There had to be an understanding between my girls and myself that my first reaction would never be a great one. They will have to brace themselves for a horrible response, and once I cool down, we could talk it through.

One of the most horrible responses I can remember

was when my daughter asked me what my reaction would be if they were using drugs. This triggered me immediately as it was always a huge fear. My response was "If I ever found out that you were using drugs, I would cut off your hand and slap you with it." They of course "told on me" to their grandparents who called me to scold me. I understand that now as an activated amygdala.

The amygdala also confuses the hippocampus causing the brain to process and store these memories on your desktop home page in your brain. Now, when something happens that reminds you of that specific memory, the memory returns and brings back the emotions you felt that day.

This discussion is always mind blowing to my clients when they hear it for the first time. In my theory, Trauma is also a perception. What could be a traumatic memory to one person, could be an unfeeling event to another. This doesn't determine weakness (of the person who filed it as traumatic), rather it determines the person's activation at the specific moment. When I participated in my EMDR training, trainees practiced on each other. I was scared that nothing would come up for me as I have an ACEs score of two. I grew up in a good family and we were raised in the church. (The science behind ACEs states that the higher the score increases the risk of disparities. My score is low.) The bilateral stimulation in EMDR activates your misplaced traumatic memories (that your hippocampus put on the homepage of your brain) and the first memory that I re-lived during the process was learning how to ride a bike.

> *I remember begging my dad at age four to teach me how to ride a bike because the neighborhood boy would ride his bike to my house, and I wanted to play with him. My dad put me on the bike (no helmet, nothing) and pushed me down our driveway's steep hill. Because of the incline, I made it to the bottom of the hill in seconds and crashed. I remember crying because my knee was scraped and my dad grabbed me and the bike and went back to the top of the driveway again. He told me, it hurts to fall, so if you don't want to fall, then learn to ride. I was so determined not to fall that I did learn how to ride the second time around. Coincidentally, that's also how I learned to swim.*

At that moment during the EMDR training, I didn't realize how traumatic that was for me. I also made the connection to my fear of heights and how I also never taught my own kids how to ride bikes. I made a comparison of my "traumatic" event that came up for me at that time the trauma of my peers and I was embarrassed (even though I had no control of what would come up). It was an unprocessed stress induced event in which I wasn't allowed to feel fear, I had to bury it and it turned into a traumatic memory. Trauma lingo speaks of Little T's and Big T's, which help people understand that small things such as riding a bike can affect the brain in the same way as something major like abuse. The severity of the dysfunction and disparity may not be the same, but the mis-process in the brain is similar.

I am by no means an expert in any of this, I just constantly re-create or add to my perceptions as I continue to practice. The newest addition to my perception is the connection to Erik Erikson's stages of psychosocial development and ACEs. Erikson's stages show how social interaction and relationships play a role in development.

To summarize for context, there are nine stages: Trust vs Mistrust (birth to 18 months), Autonomy vs Shame and Doubt (2-3 years), Initiative vs Guilt (3-5 years), Industry vs Inferiority (6-11 years), Identity vs Role confusion (12-18 years), Intimacy vs Isolation (19-40 years), Generativity vs Stagnation (40-65 years), and Ego Integrity vs Despair (65-death) [1]

My understanding of his stages is that through positive social experiences in each stage, a person is tested through conflict and how they respond determines the mastery of that stage. Each person needs to master a stage to move onto the next. I don't challenge the school of thought as it is logical, but if each stage precedes the next chronologically, if they

[1] Jeremy Sutton, Erik Erikson's Stage of Psychosocial Development Explained. (Positivepsychology.com, 2021)

don't master the first stage and gain trust, then how do they master anything after that? It seems to me that you need that one piece to even have a chance at anything else.

It's possible that a person can go through three of the stages, and then a traumatic event happens, and it could either create a blockage for the next five stages or erase the mastery of the three they gained. It's also possible, for example that a child in utero of an abused mother also experienced trauma in utero and would never master trust. If this is a true statement, that child would suffer from mistrust, shame and doubt, guilt, inferiority, role confusion, isolation, stagnation, and despair as an adult. However, it is also possible that resilient people can adapt and learn skills based on appropriate social context, but someone in an activated mode will always regress back to their natural self.

> *For example, a client never developed trust and struggled with all the other developmental stages, but she learned "skills" to mimic what the trusting behaviors should look like to adapt to society. Her natural self would always question whether her husband would leave her. She developed the "skill" to not use healthy behaviors like trying to leave him first or checking his phone to see if he was cheating on her or lying to her. However, whenever she was activated, her natural self would take over and she would threaten to leave and do things to hurt him*

intentionally.

Your natural self is simply where you are most comfortable. Your improved self is the skills you learn to mask your flaws.

> *I am naturally messy and unorganized. I drive my husband crazy as he is very structured and neat. To respect him and maintain harmony in the household, I have learned skills to mask these flaws. I must force myself to pick up and clean up. When he is on a trip, I don't do these things until the day before he comes home, this is my natural self.*

I often hear my adult clients admit that they feel immature because they can't handle their shit or control their emotions. In pairing the consequences of ACEs and the stages of development, trauma is directly connected to the perception of maturity level (broken frontal lobe) and creates the DRAMA brain.

3 DRAMA BRAIN VS EVOLVED BRAIN

The DRAMA Brain is your brain's natural shield. I call it the DRAMA Brain because that what it causes in your life. It works for you and against you at the same time. It works for you by protecting you from the hurt and pain that some events and memories can cause. However, it ends up creating traumatic memories that are misfiled in your brain and cause you to lose your shit when it connects to familiar situations in the present.

The DRAMA Brain thrives in chaos and sends out three antiheroes that can work independently or collaboratively to create the "Ultimate Peacock". In this state, all the antiheroes have the sole purpose of creating drama, activating drama, or immersing you in drama. This creates distractions to separate you from feeling and sitting in your own shit.

Antihero Manstrum (males) or Menstrum (females):

This antihero appears when expectations (created by you) are not met. This causes disappointment to turn into a personal attack on yourself. Basically, a temper tantrum is released and this Manstrum or Menstrum turns into rage, yelling, screaming, throwing, and breaking stuff and unfortunately sometimes physically harming someone or themselves. Another response could be a scary "shut down" of yourself as you focus on your own negative cognitions and allow it to stew. Every response (including shut down) intends to instill fear and cause a physical or emotional space between you and the rest of the world. This creates a false sense of power (as it is perceived that you have lost power) and a projection of control onto others.

Antihero Succubus:

This antihero uses negative reinforcement to attempt to create an outcome they want. They will withhold emotion (the emotional freeze), ignore the target (cold shoulder), withhold sex (in relationships), and use physical materials or financial means to get their way. The intention is to "break" them into submissiveness and gain a false sense of power and control. This is most seen in domestic violence and toxic relationships.

Antihero The Peacock:

This antihero is the master of distraction.

I watched a video about a peacock in the Serengeti. All the animals including predators were sitting around the water hole. Instead of humbly entering the water hole, the peacock announces its presence. He makes an entrance with his loud screaming and fans out his huge feathers. Rather than be cautious, the peacock is bold and flares out to try and create the illusions that he is bigger and more threatening than he is. In the video, after this brief performance of dominance, the lion sneaks up behind him in attempt to eat him. The peacock then shrivels back up and flies onto a high tree. From the safety of the tree, he is still screaming.

The EVOLVED BRAIN

The EVOLVED Brain is our superpower, one that is gained through experience. It creates heroes that work for us to reach resolution. It breaks down the natural shield, allows us to sit in our shit and feel what we feel in an inactivated state to reach the realistic perception of each memory. When we are activated, the frontal lobe is in dysfunction and the DRAMA Brain is in control, the traumatic memory creates a perception of victimization. The EVOLVED Brain breaks down the shield created by the DRAMA Brain helps us reprocess from a clearer perspective – just as in my pathetic traumatic memory of learning to ride a bike.

In recent years, my dad and I were sitting around the dining table, and I brought up the experience. My dad laughed and his response was "you learned how to ride a bike didn't you?" He continued to share how he was proud of that moment because I learned in seconds, and I had overcome the fear. His memory of the situation was a totally different perception than mine was because he was not activated by the event. That memory for him was a good memory and he processed it and filed it away appropriately in his hippocampus.

The EVOLVED Brain has two heroes working for us, The Orca, and the Rhino. The automatic response of being in EVOLVED Brain, is an interjection from the DRAMA Brain to return us to a false safety net.

Hero: The ORCA has learned to survive by adapting and learning. I once learned that Orcas don't automatically learn to jump over bars as you see at

SeaWorld. They are taught through positive reinforcement and the bar starts on the bottom of the tank. Each time they swim over the bar, the get rewarded. The trainers then learn to raise the bar and the Orca's adjusted to gain their positive experience, until the bar is six feet in the air, and they are catching air just to receive their reward. We can apply the progress of the Orca to our own complex situations that are, "six feet in the air."

Hero: The Rhino uses their shit as a social media platform. Rather than avoid shit, they face it head on to learn about the history of the producer. Apparently, Rhinos can tell a lot about each other's shit. The entire herd defecate in the same area, in which they visit and sit in. By sitting in and smelling other Rhino's shit, they learn about the general health, diet, age, sex, and reproductive status of each Rhino. I learned this by watching National Geographic and was fascinated. Rather than avoid the shit, they sit in it to learn. In our brain, the Rhino gives us the courage to face our own shit head on and counter the history and background of our own shit. Once we absorbed all the information that we can be in an inactivated state, we see the shit we created from an entirely different perspective, one without victimization. It then allows the traumatic memory to be filed away appropriately in our hippocampus as just a memory

In this perspective, different levels of trauma don't exist. An activating event that puts a person into the DRAMA Brain will create a blurred perspective. Imagine seeing things without glasses. Without glasses, you are unable to see clearly, and the memory goes inappropriately processed creating a traumatic memory. Unprocessed memories are traumatic memories that create dysfunction and disparities despite the judgment of the level of trauma.

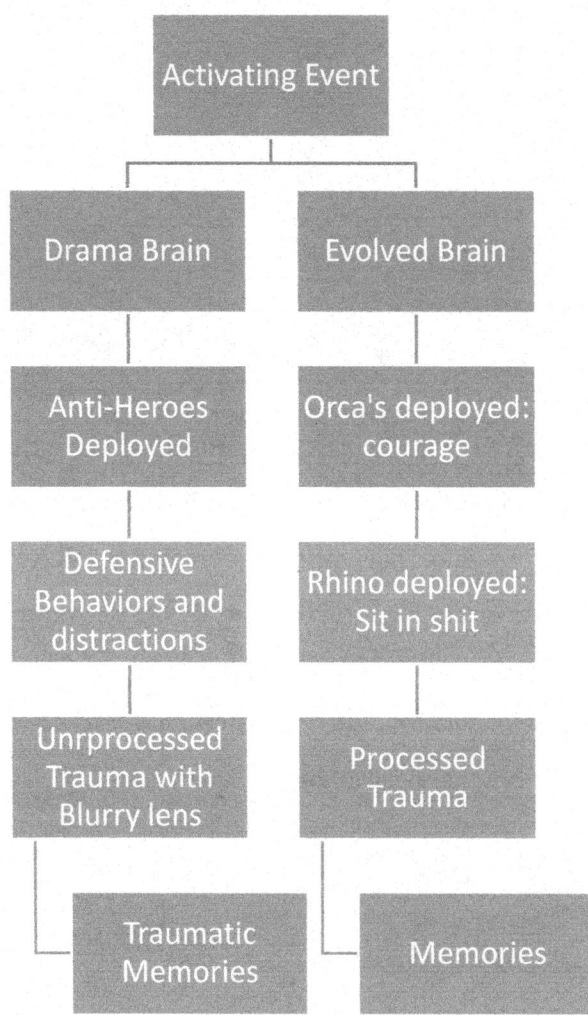

4 PANDEMIC BRAIN

In 2020, the world was hit hard with the COVID-19 pandemic. There was no cure and we watched as the virus hit like a tornado. The pandemic created a DRAMA Brain and because of the ongoing trauma, we move through or get stuck in stages comparable to Kubler-Ross' stages of grief. In an activated state, the DRAMA Brain attempts to mask our fears by creating new narratives.

Denial:

It was believed that the pandemic would blow away as quickly as it arrived. There was/is denial that our own personal bubble couldn't be affected by this global pandemic. There was/is also denial that the virus is not as widespread or as deadly as reported.

The mask mandate created a lot of controversy. Anything to do with the virus had become a political war and loyalty on which side you stood was based on the loyalty to the narrative of the party. National Republican leaders built a huge following (both socially and financially) by creating a narrative that spoke against the basic safety of using mask. Even reading this has probably triggered those who have sided with this narrative. The DRAMA brain shifts into action to defend yourself from sitting in your own shit and has now created a Peacock narrative in which I am now labeled a liberal.

Unsure of how to handle this and the panic of people being hospitalized and dying, the government put protections in place that included mask mandates, social distancing, and complete shutdowns of communities. This created fear and put everyone in DRAMA Brain.

During the pandemic, I have TikTok and other social media platforms that constantly showcased different "Karens" and "Karen" behavior. People refusing to wear masks, people defying social distancing mandates, people creating dramatic events even though there seems to be no logic to it, but they feel justified because they believe they are protecting their own freedoms. It is easier to see things from a blurred lens and feel victimized than to focus on the unknown.

My practice has grown by 60% during this time as people are spending more time together or kids are spending more time at home and begin to feel isolated. There is no denying the increase of abuse and domestic violence, the increase of substance use and the increase of anxiety and depression.

This is a direct result of the pandemic, and the unknown has put the community in an activated state. A client with a history of unhealthy relationships will increase anti-hero behaviors as the feeling of instability in the world is a reminder that activates a traumatic event that happened in the past. Oppositional defiance is a logical behavior as it reminds them of a time in their past that they felt unstable and that someone else was controlling them. They no longer feel safe or in control, so they release this anti-hero to protect them rather than focus on traumatic memory.

My cousin just texted me complaining and blaming our leadership for the state of the hospitals and schools. My cousin is a nurse in my state's largest hospital. She said that it is unacceptable that they have a tent in the parking lot holding patients and it is unacceptable that cancer surgeries are being postponed because there are no beds available. My response to her was that the accountability is left on "the herd." The fear activates and triggers society that place people in DRAMA brain.

> *I have an adult client who was rocked to her core when she found out her teenage daughter had been sneaking out of the house at night to see a boy. The rules and expectations prior were clear, which is why the teenager had to hide and sneak out. Who does the fault then point to? Is it the parent who set the boundaries or the teenager who defied it? Does there really need to be someone to blame or does blame*

create a distraction to relieve us of any personal responsibility? The teenager was feeling isolated because of the pandemic. The isolation triggered negative beliefs about herself that connected to traumatic memories from her past. Rather than feel and process what was coming up for her, she created a distraction that took her away from the crappy feelings connected to the traumatic memory. The sneaking out, filled her with adrenaline. This feeling mixed with adrenaline can be addictive. After feeling sad, her body was rushed with adrenaline that made her feel physically strong, excited, and present. Imagine what your body feels when you ride a rollercoaster, knowing the possibility of danger or the big drop makes you feel alive. Who wouldn't want to choose that feeling over sadness? The boy also became a welcomed distraction, from feeling worthless (triggered from traumatic memories and beliefs) to feeling wanted and prioritized. This became much more appealing.

The Pandemic has created my own response to immediately apply negative judgement on others. I watch in the news and social media different irrational responses of others and create "asshole" labels. Then I make the connection to these people being in DRAMA Brain. It is the only explanation as there is no logic to their behavior. In attacking people on the plane, these people clearly know the rules before they got on a plane. They also clearly know the consequences, which include a federal offense and being placed on the "no fly" list. They stand on their pedestal and dig in, despite the consequences. They justify their thinking and beliefs by connecting it to a greater cause or platform, when logically it's egocentric. Most claim it's about their freedom being infringed upon, even though they are infringing on everyone else's freedom on the plane. It's like a police chase on an island, where there is no logic and really no place to hide, it will not end well. However, they are in DRAMA Brain and have deployed all three anti-heroes to create the Ultimate peacock. This Ultimate Peacock deploys the temper tantrum, the controlling behavior, the opposition defiance, the disassociation from empathy are behaviors that explode in this state of mind. There are three things to know about dealing with someone in this mode, there will be no accountability, there is no reasoning, and they are hunting for someone to match their aggression. Deploying the Ultimate peacock is a commitment, as they will have to stay in this role or create new fears from the DRAMA they just vomited on everyone around them. There is no rationalizing with the Ultimate peacock, the only de-escalation technique is to dig in on the boundary created, which would be put on your mask or get off the plane. Matching their energy would be an unspoken challenge which will cause them to raise their energy to be heard over your voice or to be more of a peacock and spread the feathers so everyone can see. The need to feel they are in control of their lives is a basic need for them to feel safe. This creates a narrative (a picture or image) in their head on what things in their world should look and act like. When there are behaviors or people who don't match that narrative, it creates frustration at the realization of having no control over their own lives.

If I am walking into Starbucks, the schema or narrative that I created in my head includes a coffee house full of millennials on laptops, having coffee and doing their work. When I walk in now, all I see our tables pushed back, chairs taped off, and social distancing stickers on the ground. This does not match the schema I created for myself on what I thought I should see. The picture I created for myself so that I could feel safe, is destroyed my head. A new picture is created that I automatically resist as a new narrative because I need to process this change and I am reminded that I am not safe or in control. In the meantime, I am activated and escalated because this is not what I expected to see. The Peacock is ready to be deployed at any moment.

Many people have half-heartedly joked about the pandemic creating a Zombie Apocalypse. I believe there is some truth to this conspiracy theory. Not the undead coming alive, but the pandemic has activated people so much that it overloads their brains causing a detachment from reality. Since the pandemic, I have treated numerous clients who have symptoms of depersonalization disorder. They all seem to have the same descriptions. They feel as if they are in dream state, not really in their body, they feel that time is moving in slow motion, sometimes they stare at a body part (such as hand), and it grows super large. When they are in this "dream" state, they can't tell what is real and what is not. These clients also have a history of trauma prior to the pandemic. In the beginning of the pandemic, they were dealing with random suicidal ideations. Now a few are starting to teeter between suicidal ideations and homicidal ideations. This made me think. What if the people who are showing violent tendencies or behaviors in are in this "dream state" and are detached from reality? What if the pandemic has triggered a depersonalization state in which people are reacted to their tendencies in a "dream" state? The US news wrote an article written by Robert Preidt and Ernie Mundell (Oct 6, 2021) on CDC data that shows the murder rate has risen 30% during the pandemic. This has been the biggest trend jump since Sept 11, 2001.

Power and control play a huge role in one's response to change. Traumatic events play a huge role for one's need for power and control. Resiliency plays a huge role in adjustment. Three powerful statements listed above, but all true.

An event that creates a shift in perception can be traumatic. That perception is then generalized and creates a flinching response to any event that is similar. For example, a rescued dog that has been beaten by past owners will not immediately take to another person's approach. If a person lifts their hand, the dog will immediately flinch as it has attuned to the negative meaning of a raised hand. Traumatic events tend to be events that happen to you rather than events that you have control over. These traumas build up a defense system. That includes an overcompensation of trying to control whatever is in your power and irrationally trying to control things that aren't in your power (which is the source of most conflicts). For an activated person, any change in environment causes an imbalance to the structure they created for themselves. The change enables the generalization and correlation to the traumatic event(s) in which they have felt the loss of control. This puts them back to a spiral of activation and they begin to sustain themselves in survivor mode. They lash out at others to try and regain power because the loss of control has made them feel powerless. They get frustrated and try to change situations and environments that don't match their expectations. Part of the defense mechanism is creating a narrative or a plan. When someone or something doesn't match the narrative or plan, they either lash out and try to change it to fit their narrative or they just lash out in frustration.

When none of these things work and they continue to not

feel safe in their environment, defense mechanisms seem to morph into detachment. An overload of "feeling" turns into a dysfunction of not feeling. I believe this is the connection to the "dream" state.

Resiliency happens with an initial successful event that is processed to create resolution. Activation is the body's response to stress. When the stressor is resolved, your body resolves to a normal inactivated state (homeostasis). For this to happen, there must be a stressful event in the past, which was experienced through to resolution. That memory of a successful resolve of a stressful event, and the feeling of relief that came with that success provides the motivation to keep moving forward. It also combats the blurred lens effect or perception of victimization. The memory of being able to overcome conflict or the stressor in the past creates the strength to push through. This resiliency is a superpower. It creates the defining moment that moves a perception from victim to victor.

> *Recently, I fractured my knee in a soccer game. It is not the first bone I broke playing soccer, it's the 8th, not including meniscus tears in my knee. Injuring myself does not stop me from playing the exact way I have been playing since I was younger. I don't flinch, I just play the way my brain tells me too. Although the injury causes discomfort, it has not traumatized me as I felt "at home" on the field. Soccer has been my coping skill and I don't play with a "blurred*

lens". In my perception, this incident was part of the game. Past injuries and events that happened throughout my soccer life were processed appropriately and created a resilience to overcome the injury.

However, if I was in an activated state, I would have gone into DRAMA Brain and perceived the entire incident as an attack on me. I would have blamed my team for allowing it to happen, I would have tried to attack the players that were involved in my injury, and maybe even yelled at the Ref. I most likely would have never stepped foot on a soccer field again. Unfortunately for my family, I am already shopping for a new pair of soccer shoes.

5 REPETITIVE COMPULSIONS: SELF SABOTAGE

My clients always ask the same question, "why do I always do the same thing over and over?" We call it self-sabotage. In our perspective, self-sabotage is part of the DRAMA brain. An activated event causes you to go into DRAMA brain creating a blurred lens, then deploys the anti-heroes that protects you with defensive behaviors. This creates two possible narratives, the Illusion of the "do over" and/or creating an alternate reality.

The Illusion of the "do over" is driven by the lack of mastery in the event. I work with youth with promise which have not gained the skills to properly navigate through challenges. The negative beliefs take over, which normally are things like I am not good enough or a feeling of worthlessness. This then intensifies the fear of failure or shame. It then creates a sense of activation overwhelm which causes negative coping skills as distraction, avoidance and/or denial. This then leads to repetitive behavior.

The youth that I work with struggle with school. When a

significant test comes up to test their competency, they allow the negative cognitions such as "I am dumb", "I am incapable", or "I will fail to take over". They create distractions such as picking fights or immersing themselves in drama and other things to worry about. This allows the blame to be shifted to the drama and hide their perception that others will see the negative cognitions and believe it themselves. They self-sabotage and set themselves up to fail but under the guise of the drama and not because they fear being revealed as incapable, weak, or whatever negative belief they have about themselves.

The alternative reality is created when we want to normalize what happened to us. Someone who has sexual trauma might use this alternative reality to create a new normal. If sexual trauma leads to sexual promiscuity, the behavior is justified with a belief that using their body as being wanted or desired. They may also try to normalize with "digging in" to this alternative reality and having "billboard behavior". Not hiding their alternative reality but advertising it to help them believe that this is normal, and rationalizing their self-worth. It also creates a disillusion of love and/or healthy relationships. They begin to have the underlining belief that sex will fill the void they are missing and take the place of the love they are desperately seeking.

> *I have played soccer since I was six years old . The*
> *decades of playing and probably an inheritance of*

bad joint genes led me to have knee problems. I probably could benefit from surgery, but instead I slap on a knee brace, lather up in Icy hot and continue with my day. Rather than take the time to have the needed rehab and recovery, I glaze it over with temporary fixes and prolong my suffering. The prolonging of suffering is what we do emotionally when we don't allow ourselves to "Sit in our shit".

6 FACING THE UGLY TRUTH

Facing the ugly truth is the hardest part of the process and the beginning step to move forward. We hide this the part in hopes that no one will find it and we will forget about it. Instead, we allow our DRAMA Brain to take over and create alternative realities to draw attention away from the ugly truth. It reminds me of the HULK. Bruce Banner is the primary ego and when he becomes activated, he spins out of control into the HULK. As the HULK, he is allowed to smash and destroy and answer to his rage. He creates destruction and draws attention to his alter ego and the damage.

About a month and a half into the Youth Challenge program becomes a drama filled week. It is this week the test to determine if they can get into the high school diploma program like the GED. Historically, this is the week of drama, when the cadets go AWOL, and fights and chaos ensues. The high-tension week starts to activate negative cognitions and cause most to allow DRAMA Brain to take over.

One cadet once told me that she was depressed, and I asked her why. She couldn't give me an answer, then she talked about how everyone around was acting and how it was diminishing her motivation. She talked about quitting the program as it was emotionally overwhelming. Her story began to spin out as she began to find all the little things her peers did to irritate her. I stopped her after a while and asked her why she was REALLY feeling depressed. She immediately went back to bring up new drama stories. Then I casually asked her about the test this week. She then admitted that she was worried about this test. Then I asked her what the real ugly truth is, what is she really hiding that she doesn't want to say aloud? She took a breath and said, I'm afraid that I am dumb, and I won't get my high school diploma. I am ashamed that I might be the only one. I asked her if it was possible that she was creating all this drama in her head because it was easier to focus on the drama and give herself an excuse to give up. Shockingly, she was insightful and admitted it. From there we could do the real work. Guiding her to the EVOLVED Brain state allowed her to truly focus on how she felt and why she felt this way. She was able to reprocess on her own, the negative cognition and realized that she can't undo all her bad habits in

weeks and may need more time to learn how to learn.
She realized that although it would suck if she
finished the program without a degree, it didn't mean
that she would never get one.

This biggest part of the ugly truth is what I call "Sitting in Your Shit". Unprocessed events lead back to traumatic memories in which our brains are trained to hide and protect. We must map our way back to the source, then process that original traumatic memory to release the negative beliefs. This is the most difficult part of the process as it has all "The Feels", and it doesn't feel good. Prior to my revelation, I would focus on coping skills and distractions, which were just band aids and possibly creating more dysfunction. Now my saying is "Feel what you feel".

Most of my clients will talk about how they hate crying and how feeling that vulnerable makes them feel and look weak. However, when you map it out logically, it takes strength to break down the walls to be vulnerable. It takes strength to allow yourself to sit in your shit and feel. Logically, it's stronger to show and acknowledge emotions than hide it.

Ignoring the fracture in my knee doesn't make it
stronger, in fact it could make it worse. Applying the
brace and walking on crutches allows it to heal.
When the bone does finally heal, the calcium fortified
bone becomes stronger than the rest. The healing
process of my knee is like the healing process of our

life events. I can't rush my healing process. I asked my doctor when I could start playing again. He wouldn't give me a definite date and based it on my healing and physical therapy. When I regain full motion and strength in my quads, is when I can work myself up to playing again.

The emotional healing process also can't be rushed. There is no timeline as everyone processes differently and at their own pace.

7 WHATS NEXT

"Be a Rhino and sit in your shit" seems like the most idiotic advice ever. However, if you break down the process it makes more sense to the point of labeling it common. Once the Rhino stage is reached, the stagnation diminishes. A memory or an emotion comes up and our immediate reaction would be to try and create distraction because the emotion is unwanted. We must fight the initial reaction to swat it away and allow ourselves to Sit in the shit.

Step 1: Identify the emotion. The original emotion may not be the primary emotion. The original or current emotion is a distraction from the primary emotion because of the negative cognition that we created ourselves that makes us believe that emotions are a sign of weakness. A primary emotion normally is basic, "my feelings were hurt", "I am afraid", or "it didn't match my schema" (my expectation of what it should look like) and "I'm disappointed".

Most of my client's first reaction is anger and rage. When I help them process, it is difficult to get beyond

41

"I am angry" because admitting that you are hurt is weakness. Once we face the ugly truth, they go to "It hurt my feelings because...". Then we can move on to step 2.

Step 2: Based on the primary emotion, what trauma or negative event does this situation remind you of? Recall that negative event or traumatic memory. Replay it in your mind. Notice and acknowledge the emotions and allow yourself to feel it.

Step 3: What is the negative cognition about me that came out of this event? What did it lead me to believe about myself? What were /are the emotions that are connected to these beliefs? Looking back as the person I am at this very moment, what are the rational or logical beliefs about the situation. What are the rational or logical beliefs about me?

Recently, I was helping a client process a recent death in her family and the personal guilt that came with the death. She has been in Youth Challenge Academy, away from her family when she found out that her uncle (who was a father figure to her) passed away. She didn't tell anyone as she fears showing emotion. She believes that it is a sign of weakness. Instead, she allowed herself to be triggered and started a fight with someone because they were teasing a fellow cadet. She identified her current emotion as anger but became honest with herself and stated it reminded her of a time when boys had called her names and she felt worthless. She didn't want her friend to feel that way. We processed that event to where she realized that although the feelings about this incident were real and valid, it came down to the guilt she was feeling because her uncle passed away. The last words that she told her uncle was that he just wanted her to go away, because he supported her being put in the program. The emotion connected to this event was hurt and it made her feel worthless, the same emotion connected to the being called names by the boys in her past (which led to a past suicide attempt). The negative cognition is interwoven between different events but connected through a spiderweb of similar negative cognitions.

In the end, she was able to rationalize that she believes her uncle was a man of God and was in heaven. This led her to rationalize that he could see her now and could understand her heart. It also gave her motivation to keep moving forward on this path. However, that was only the beginning of her process. The next day, we had planned a butterfly release for all the females as a handful of them have lost family members recently. During the butterfly release she stood on the side of the building and wept continuously. She wept for two hours following the release. In processing this moment with her, she spoke about how she was forced to feel and sit in her shit. I told her what a beautiful moment it was for her, because she was able to feel and release some of that grief. We talked about how often she holds back the feelings and then Peacocks and creates negative events with her peers or self-harms. We also discussed the percentage (to give her a measurement) of process that she was at, in which she stated 40% We both agreed that this was the farthest process she has every obtained in her lifetime.

Step 4: Reflection. What were the irrational thoughts versus the rational thoughts? What would "Present and Current You" say to "Past you" in this moment? Basically, based on the person you are now re-examining the situation from the past, what would you say to your victimized self in the past? A letter to yourself is a powerful tool to reach resolution. I often have my clients write a letter from the perspective of the person they are in this moment to the person they were in the traumatic memory. Through growth and experience, we are not the same people we were in the past as we continue to evolve. We are often kinder to other people than to ourselves. Separating the "past you" from the "current you", provides the detachment needed to allow a path for forgiveness and rational positive cognitions.

In working with a child who experienced sexual trauma. We processed the trauma through brain spotting and EMDR. As her brain continues to process the trauma, I taught her how to do sit in it rather than container it (We put it in a virtual container until the next therapy session). She shared how she was in school, and her private parts started to throb painfully like when we were in session processing her trauma. She shared how she went into the bathroom to just breathe and regain her power over the situation. She challenged her irrational thoughts which were causing the somatic sensation by saying "This isn't real" and remembering the positive cognition during EMDR "It is not my fault" made the sensation stop. This 8-year-old was able to do what adults fail to do consistently. She was able to face her emotions, her trauma, and work through it.

However, to solidify resolution, I had her do two assignments. The First assignment was to write a letter to her "Bad Uncle" and write what you would want to tell him now that she has processed everything. The second assignment was to write a letter as the person she is at this moment to the 5-year-old that was treated badly by "Bad Uncle". In both letters, she spoke about feeling safe now. She has no blurred lens because she is no longer activated.

8 THE THERAPEUTIC RELATIONSHIP

Some clients believe that therapy is a venting session. This is true to a point, but once a therapeutic relationship is established, a good therapist will challenge your beliefs and intentions. There is no timeline for this process, and we can't give you a number of sessions in which you will reach resolution. For therapy to work effectively, you as the client will have to be ready to be a client. The therapist is not a magician and there is no magic pill, believe me I am still looking for one. I often tell my clients that therapy is a marathon and not a sprint. We move at the client's pace, and I would never force a client to talk about something they are not ready to discuss. This is especially important for clients with trauma, they need to feel as if they have control over their sessions.

A lot of first-time clients sign up for therapy and come into the first session with anxiety. It's a whole new relationship and one that should exist with vulnerability. Clients who have experienced trauma in their past, don't like surprises.

Not knowing what will happen creates anxiety.

There are 4 basic negative cognitions with starting with a new therapist. Will the therapist think I'm crazy or confirm my beliefs that I am. Will the therapist judge me and think I am a bad person? A big negative cognition is really the fear of vulnerability, what will I have to talk about? In my own personal experience, my biggest fear was if the therapist will be a good fit for me.

A therapist that is a good fit for you would be someone that you connect with in the first session. Someone who makes you feel safe, and you feel that you could eventually trust. A good therapist would never tell you what to do or solve your problem for you. This is a dangerous situation as that therapist is taking responsibility over your life. Therapy is a partnership, there is no hierarchy. I would never validate my clients by saying that I am proud of them, this instills the belief that I have ownership over the client's behaviors. This also creates a hierarchal relationship in which the client could try to keep pleasing the therapist, and resist sharing information that could damage this validation.

Building rapport is an important part of the therapeutic relationship, as this helps build trust and allows vulnerability. Rapport looks like a natural conversation in which you can feel safe. It's a space in which you can have a voice and feel validated. I introduce a trust scale from 1-10. Level 1 is no trust. Clients can only share surface information and not provide detail. At level 6, clients can discuss conflicts or traumas that are less significant. They are insightful and able to admit and see flaws in themselves. They can accept a different perspective and may even be ready to attempt small changes. Level 10 is total trust, and the client is ready to be vulnerable and is ready to discuss or process any event. Every session we determine the trust level, this gives me a baseline for the next session. Clients know that at any time, they can press the freeze button. The freeze button allows the client to advocate for themselves that they are not able to discuss or want to discuss certain events at that moment.

Level 1	No trust built, only surface information
Level 2	Able to discuss current stressors, but not really to share real feelings and emotions
Level 3	Able to talk about relationships and behaviors, but not ready to hear feedback
Level 4	Is open to answering questions when asked but will not voluntarily provide information
Level 5	Shares more information without being prompted.
Level 6	Ready to discuss less significant traumas, receives feedback and thinks about possible changes.
Level 7	Starts to implement small changes, shares more information, and begins to ask for feedback
Level	Able to discuss emotions and the connection to past traumas. Breezes over traumas as

8	insignificant details.
Level 9	Able to recognize they have trauma that directly affects their beliefs and behaviors.
Level 10	Able to process trauma and begins to process trauma on their own. Full vulnerability, talks the entire session without being prompted.

Change is solely the client's responsibility. The therapist supports the change and holds the client responsible to their own goals. For example, if a client is frustrated about the lack of motivation in themselves, a therapist might bring up the client's use of marijuana and the direct negative effect it has on motivation. When new clients make statements like "I had so many therapists in the past and therapy has never worked for me." My response is "Is it possible that you weren't ready to change until now?" Therapy doesn't work if you use it as something you do to check off the box that you tried. Therapy is commitment to yourself, that you want a different perspective from a non-biased outsider. You want someone who will challenge your beliefs and actions and basically call you out on your shit.

At Family Tree Project, we interview clients before we accept them. We normally don't take court ordered clients unless they are committed to change and want to be in therapy. We don't take clients that are just looking to check off the boxes, because our investment in our client matches their investment in themselves. Trauma focused therapy is not brief interventions.

There must be a level of readiness for a client to benefit from therapy. If there is internal motivation to change, but no level of trust, a therapist can work with this. A good therapist will be patient and allow time for building rapport and trust. A good therapist will also attune to your energy and will know when you are feeling "off". The therapist will know based off your "off" energy when to back off and when to push forward. I often ask my clients when they are in DRAMA brain, "what is it that you need from me today?". This always throws them off their platform and stops the ranting for a second. I ask them "Do you need me to just sit here, listen and validate you?" or "do you need me to listen and challenge you?" Every single time, the client will change their mode and let me know they need me to challenge their thoughts and then I can help move them into EVOLVED brain.

> *I use the term "punch you in the face", it's a virtual punch that may sting a bit as it goes against the current perception. I warn the client and give them the option to hear it. "Are you ready for a punch in the face or shall I keep it to myself?" Every single time, the client will agree to brace for the virtual punch.*

This pivotal moment is the agreement between the

therapist and the client to prepare to move from DRAMA brain to EVOLVED brain. This gives them control over the feedback they receive and prepares them for information that might challenge their current beliefs. When they agree to the punch in the face, they are more accepting and ready for the feedback.

Although working through and processing trauma can be exhausting. Most clients end up enjoying therapy and are excited for their next session. Of course, these clients are the ones that reach Level 10. Everyone moves at their own pace, there is no judgment. As therapists, we are honored to be part of the journey to healing.

9. CONCLUSION

I watched the Netflix original, the Squid games. All of players live every hour not knowing if they will live the next. They go through every hour not knowing if someone will betray or kill them. It created a detachment from emotions as other players die right in front of them. This created a moment of relief for them as they could take a breath for just a second. It also created homicidal ideations as they realize there could only be one winner. At any moment, someone could make the decision to eliminate them. It was important not to seem weak, because that would make them easy prey. Metaphorically, we are living in the squid games as the pandemic stretches on. The constant instability of not knowing or not being able to control our own safety is causing dysfunction in individuals and in our communities.

Lately, I've been struggling with the idea behind seeing something and saying something. When it comes to terrorist attacks or other threatening events, this seems to be the saying that goes behind it. As a clinician, if you are seeing a very disturbing trend, do you say something and make noise? In conversations with my business partner (who is also a clinician), we have been discussing this ethical dilemma. If we know that something bad is happening and we aren't saying anything, does it go against are ethics? Why is it so scary to say something and make noise? If someone proves me wrong, then that's a good thing. If we create awareness, then maybe we save a life. This book, is the first firecracker and it is just the beginning.

Either use this book to understand, so that you can seek help in working through your perceptions and sitting in your own shit, or use this book to spread the word and practice your own process until you are ready to seek help. Therapy only works with transparency on both sides.

THE FAMILY TREE PROJECT STORY

I started the Family Tree Project in 2014 right before I was licensed. I developed a Family Strengthening curriculum during my post grad experience and through Happenstance, it got into the hands of the Domestic Violence Action Center. They contacted me through a colleague and offered to buy it. I immediately copyrighted it and applied for a business license. I offered to implement the curriculum with grant money. We called the curriculum "The Family Tree Project". My past Partners and I received three grants to work with families and provide these services. During the first phase, one of my Partners and myself got licensed. We decided to place our private practice under the Family Tree Project's current license. Through a partnership with my friend's non-profit, we were able to have a space to provide therapy and implement the program. It was through this seed money that we eventually grew into the practice we are today.

The process wasn't easy as we lacked financial stability which understandably took it's toll financial on other partners. Family Tree Project wouldn't be where we are today without the original founders, Baylene Thompson and Lisa Chun Fat. I would not have had the courage to build a practice alone and I owe that to them. I also probably wouldn't have made it through grad school without their support as they were my battle buddies. I will be forever grateful to their contributions to my life and to the practice.

Our vision and mission that we created back then remains the same as it is now. We believe in helping those who want help. We don't turn anyone away because they lack insurance or financial ability. Till this day, we hold a pro-bono client load that varies between 20-30%. We also believe in giving students in the field a better experience then we had. Many of our students have become employees and have since been licensed and moved on to their own careers.

ABOUT THE AUTHOR

This is the hardest part of the book to write. I am born and raised on Oahu, Hawaii. I have been married to the cleanest and neatest man in America, Zan. He annoys me daily, but till this day, he still makes me laugh out loud. His lack of understanding (or even motivation to learn) of Psychology, forces me to be a wife and mother at home and not a therapist. We have 2 young adult daughters, in which they are proof that there is a positive change after puberty. Puberty seems like forever, but before you call an exorcist, they do eventually calm down. I'm still not the coolest mom in the world, but I am now tolerable. I appreciate every moment I have with all of them.